UNDERSTANDING THE WESTERN SCHISM

PHILLIP CAMPBELL

ISBN: 978-1-957206-28-8
Cover: The dispute of the popes (14th century miniature, Bibliothèque nationale de France)

Published by

Cruachan Hill Press
12552 E Michigan Ave.
Grass Lake, MI 49240
www.cruachanhill.com

Printed and Bound in the United States of America

TABLE OF CONTENTS

Introduction: Understanding the Western Schism

The Western Schism of 1378-1417 is something that plenty of people are vaguely aware of, but few know the details about. We've all heard about that one time back in the Middle Ages when there were two (or maybe was it three?) men simultaneously claiming to be pope and excommunicating one another. For most people, this is where their knowledge of the Western Schism ends.

But there is so much more to understand about this remarkable period in Catholic history. What brought the Western Schism about? Why did it go on for so long? What effects did this schism have on the Church? And for that matter, what is a schism, anyway? By what criteria does the Church judge if a claimant to the papacy is legitimate or not? What lessons for today can we take away from the Western Schism?

In this booklet, we will attempt to sort through these questions to give you a better understanding of this strange and fascinating epoch in Church history. We will begin by considering the concept of schism in general and then move on to the details of the Western Schism in particular.

What is Schism?

Unity is one of the essential marks of the Church. In the Creed we recite every Sunday at Mass, we profess belief in "One, Holy, Catholic, and Apostolic Church." This oneness is integral to the Church's identity. Our Lord Jesus Christ taught that this unity was the same unity shared between the Father and the Son within the Holy Trinity, and that this oneness is itself a sign of the Church's divine origin. In the Gospel of John, He says:

> I do not pray for these only, but also for those who believe in me through their word, that they may all be one; even as thou, Father, art in me, and I in thee, that they also may be in us, so that the world may believe that thou hast sent me. The glory which thou hast given me I have given to them, that they may be one even as we are one, I in them and thou in me, that they may become perfectly one, so that the world may know that thou hast sent me and hast loved them even as thou hast loved me. (John 17:20-23, RSVCE)

The *Catechism of the Catholic Church*, furthermore, tells us that this unity is expressed in certain bonds that tie all Catholics together. Examples of these bonds of unity include profession of the same faith, celebration of the same sacraments, and the descent of our clergy from one apostolic succession (CCC 815).

This is why from the earliest days of Christianity, Christians have viewed it as a particularly grievous thing to wound the unity of the Church. In the New Testament, St. Paul admonished the Ephesians that "there is one body and one Spirit...one Lord, one faith, one baptism, one God and Father of us all, who is above all and through all and in all." (Eph. 4:4-6). Elsewhere he warned that there should be "no division in the body" (1. Cor. 12:25) and that Christians should avoid those who stir up division (Tit. 3:10). To divide the Church is to sin against the unity for God's people willed by Jesus Christ.

Those who split or divide the Church commit the sin of *schism*. Schism comes from the Greek word *skhisma*, which means a "cleft" or "division." The Church Fathers were fond of imagining the oneness of the Church like the seamless garment of Christ (cf. John 19:23); they imagined schism as ripping or tearing apart this seamless garment. This is why the Church Fathers earnestly stressed the importance of unity. Consider this passage from the African martyr, St. Cyprian of Carthage:

> The Church is also one, though spread far and wide by its ever-increasing fruitfulness. There are many rays of the sun, but one light. There are many branches of a tree, but one strength from its mighty root. From one spring flow many streams, and though they are multiplied in rich abundance, yet they are still united in one source. You cannot separate a ray of light from the sun, because its unity does not allow division. You can break a branch from a tree, but when broken, it will not be able to bud. Cut a stream off from its source and it dries up. It is the same with the Church. Filled with the light of the Lord, it shines its rays over the whole world, yet everywhere it is one and the same light that shines, and the body is not divided. [1]

How is the Sin of Schism Committed?

To understand schism, we must first understand that schism is a sin, but it is also a canonical status. We will consider each in turn.

The sin of schism is committed whenever a Catholic disassociates himself from the Church by withdrawing submission from the lawful ecclesiastical authorities, but without repudiating Catholicism altogether. The *Catechism of the Catholic Church* defines it as "the refusal of submission to the Roman Pontiff or of communion with the members of the Church subject to him" (CCC 2089). Committing the sin of schism is more than just ignoring a rule or disobeying an order; it is the withdrawal of submission and a denial of the Church's authority. In other words, the schismatic seeks to carve out an independent niche for himself outside of the Church's ecclesiastical structure and against the express direction of the Church's authorities, disregarding its jurisdiction. The *Catechism* classifies schism as a sin against the virtue of faith and a sin against the First Commandment (CCC 2089).

Those who persist in committing the sin of schism may also be guilty of the canonical crime of schism. To be in the canonical state of schism means that one incurs automatic excommunication, per the *Code of Canon Law* (CIC 1364); in other words, one declared schismatic is considered outside the Church. A recent example of this is the case of Archbishop Carlo Maria Viganò, former nuncio to the United States. Viganò had denied the validity of Pope Francis's election and refused a summons to Rome to explain himself and was subsequently declared in schism by the Dicastery for the Doctrine of the Faith in 2024.

Entire groups can also go into schism. An example is furnished by the 2016 case of the Universal Christian Church of the New Jerusalem (UCCNJ). The UCCNJ began in 1947 in Italy, centered on the apparitions made to a certain Giuseppina Norcia. As often happens in such cases, the content of the apparitions was bizarre, but the strange doctrines of the UCCNJ do not concern us here, save one: their denial of papal authority based on their view that the UCCNJ constitutes the "real Church" and that the Catholic Church is not recognized by God.[2] After decades of back and forth, on July 5, 2016, the Bishop of the Diocese of Sora, Gerardo Antonazzo, declared the group in schism. In a formal communication from the diocese, which was read from every pulpit, Bishop Antonazzo invoked Canon 1364, stating that "all the faithful who this 'self-styled Church' are punished with *latae sententiae* [i.e., automatic] excommunication for the canonical crime of schism."[3]

During the first millennium, the Greek speaking churches of the East were frequently in schism with the Latin speaking churches of the West. The Antiochian Schism (362-414), Acacian Schism (484-519), the Schism of the Three Chapters (553-698) and the Photian Schism (863-867) are the most notable examples. The causes for these schisms were varied, but often had to do with conflicts between the authority of the Byzantine emperors and the popes. History's most famous schism is the Great Schism of 1054, which saw the final break between the Church of Rome and the Church of Constantinople, a regrettable sundering of Christian unity which has yet to be repaired.

Schism is always a tragedy for the Church as it obscures the unity promised by Jesus Christ, confuses the faithful, and leads souls astray.

What are Antipopes?

Historically, one of the greatest occasions for schism was during a contested papal election. For example, in the year 251, during a period of persecution, the Church of Rome was deeply split on the issue of whether to be lenient or severe with Christians who had lapsed under persecution. The Roman clergy divided into two sects—the majority elected a man named Cornelius, but a smaller sect of rigorists held a separate election and chose a man named Novatian, who was against reconciling lapsed sinners. The Church thus had two men simultaneously claiming to be pope.

There can, of course, only be one pope. In the above case, the entire Church recognized Cornelius as the legitimate pope, with the exception of a small minority who shared Novatian's ideas. Novatian was not recognized as pope and today is known as an *antipope*, that is, one who falsely claims to be pope in opposition to a legitimately elected pope. In this example, the Antipope Novatian was the leader of what has become known as the Novatian Schism.

Sometimes antipopes were propped up by civil authorities hostile to the Church. In 1159, Pope Alexander III was opposed by an antipope who took the title Victor IV. Antipope Victor was supported by the Holy Roman Emperor, Frederick Barbarossa. Victor took control of Rome by violence and expelled Alexander III. Victor had an entire duplicate papal court, with his own cardinals and curial staff. When Victor died, he was replaced by two other antipopes, Paschal III and Callixtus III, until the schism finally ended in 1178 when Callixtus abandoned his claims and submitted to Alexander III.[4]

The Holy Roman Emperor Frederick Barbarossa (r. 1155-1190) supported multiple antipopes against the Pope Alexander III

Throughout the Church's history, there have been around 40 antipopes. Antipopes and schism often go hand in hand, as the antipope is, by definition, the leader of a schismatic sect which refuses to recognize the authority of the legitimate pope.

How does one tell who is the legitimate pope and who is the antipope? Generally this is easy, as the antipopes were not usually elected through the normal processes established by the Church. Often they were pushed by heretical sects, propped up by monarchs, or seized power by brute force. Occasionally, however, there were circumstances when it was not immediately clear who the true pope was. The Western Schism was one such instance.

Now that we have spent some time laying the groundwork for understanding schisms and antipopes, let us move on to discuss the Western Schism in particular.

The Western Schism

The Western Schism began in 1378 and lasted until 1417. During those thirty-nine years, nine different individuals claimed to hold the papal office representing three distinct lines of popes, or "obediences," as they were then called. Of those nine claimants, four were antipopes. The schism unfolded in several stages over the decades. We will consider each in turn. To begin, we must go back to 1309 when the popes abandoned Rome and moved to Avignon.

The Avignon Papacy

In 1305, Raymond Bertrand de Got, Archbishop of Bourdeaux, was elected Pope Clement V. A Frenchman who owed his election to the influence of French bishops and the

French monarchy. Clement was not enthused about leaving France to take up residence in Rome, which had a reputation as an unruly, crime-ridden city dominated by murderous factions in pay of the local political families. In 1309, Clement decided to settle his papal court at Avignon, a papal city located within French territory. Though technically part of the Papal States, Avignon was culturally French. It allowed Clement to technically move into papal territory while remaining within in the comforts of the French culture he knew and loved.

Situating the papacy in Avignon gave the kings of France considerable influence over the affairs of the Church. Clement's administration was staffed by Frenchmen, and Clement was popularly perceived as a creature of the French monarch.

This situation endured for sixty-eight years and spanned the reigns of seven popes. During these long years the Avignon Papacy earned a reputation for corruption and political favoritism towards the French. Many reform-minded clergy and religious urged the popes to end the scandal of the Avignon Papacy and return the papal court to Rome. The popes resisted this, however, as the turbulence of Rome made it an undesirable city to live in.

The Papal Conclave of 1378

The last Avignon pope, Gregory XI (r. 1370-1378), faced increasing pressure from friends, political allies, and eminent figures to return to Rome—most notably, from St. Catherine of Siena, who wrote the pope fourteen letters encouraging his return. Gregory finally decided to return the papacy to Rome. There was some controversy about the move; the French king and French bishops strongly opposed it, as they feared they would lose their influence over the papal court. Gregory was resolute, however, and in January of 1378 he returned the papal court to Rome.

But Gregory XI did not long survive the return, dying only two months after his entry into Rome. A new pope needed to be chosen. After sixty-eight years of French popes, the people of Rome were insistent that the cardinals elect a Roman who would remain in Rome. The great families of Rome orchestrated a campaign of popular protest to put pressure on the cardinals to select an Italian. Accordingly, the cardinals elected Bartolomo Prignano, Archbishop of Bari, as Pope Urban VI in April 1378.

The cardinals immediately regretted their decision, however, for Urban proved a determined reformer who preached against their excesses and luxuries. The French cardinals soon left Rome and congregated at Anagni, where they summoned Urban to a meeting. Pope Urban refused to attend; he knew he was unpopular with the cardinals and feared he would be imprisoned or slain. When Urban refused to present himself, the cardinals declared him deposed and elected a replacement—Robert of Geneva, a Frenchman who took the name Clement VII. The cardinals justified their actions by arguing that the election of Urban VII was made under duress due to the pressure of the Roman mob and was therefore invalid.

Following some skirmishes between supporters of Clement and Urban, Clement realized he could not seize Rome. He and the French cardinals returned to Avignon, where they were welcomed and protected by the French monarch, King Charles V.

Thus began the Western Schism. There were now two popes, one in Rome and one in Avignon, each who had been elected by an assembly of cardinals. We shall henceforth speak of the Roman obedience and the Avignon obedience when discussing the respective claimants of each line.

Two Obediences

The manner by which the pope is selected has varied throughout the centuries. In ancient times the pope was typically chosen by a vote of the Roman clergy or could even be chosen by popular acclamation. Later, the Holy Roman Emperors exercised considerable control over who could hold the papal chair, often nominating candidates or vetoing those they deemed unacceptable. In 1059, Pope Nicholas II issued the papal bull *In nomine Domini*, establishing the papal conclave system as we now know it, in which a pope is selected by a vote of the College of Cardinals.

But how many cardinals need to be present to elect a pope? Are the cardinals allowed to negate their votes if they believe they voted in error or under duress? Do the cardinals have the right to declare that a pope has lost the papal office? These questions were all part of the controversy surrounding the Western Schism.

The Western Schism gave rise to two papal lines called "obediences"—rival papal courts which each had their own College of Cardinals, their own curial officials, which promulgated their own decrees, and minted their own coins. They even issued excommunications against one another.

Because of the special place the Church held in medieval society, who held the papal office was not just a spiritual matter; kings, too, took sides in the dispute and aligned their resources behind their favored claimants. The kingdom of France, of course, supported Clement VII and

The Palais de Papes at Avignon, the fortress where the Avignon line of popes kept their court

the Avignon line, as did Aragon, Castile, and the Kingdom of Naples in southern Italy. England, Poland, the Low Countries, and the Papal States, meanwhile, supported the Roman obedience. Rival kingdoms tended to support rival claimants: Scotland supported Avignon while its enemy England supported Rome, and Portugal was loyal to Rome while its enemy Aragon pledged itself to Avignon. Meanwhile the Holy Roman Empire (Germany), because of its great diversity of little duchies and member states, did not fully commit to either claimant.

The schism also aggravated factionalism within local communities. For example, when leaders of the Flemish city of Bruges went over to the Avignon obedience in 1382, there was an exodus of tradesmen out of the city, as most of them supported the Roman Pope Urban and wished to ply their trades in an "Urbanist" city where the atmosphere would be friendlier. The leaders of Bruges, meanwhile accused the Urbanists of being heretics.[5]

The saints, too, were divided in their allegiance. The Roman line was supported by St. Catherine of Siena, St. Catherine of Sweden, and Bl. Ursulina of Parma, among others. The Avignon line, meanwhile, counted St. Vincent Ferrer, St. Colette, and Bl. Pierre of Luxembourg among its supporters. Some eminent clergymen alternately supported both lines. For example, the French Cardinal Philip of Alençon initially supported Clement VII before switching his allegiance to Urban VI.

The universities, as well, were divided along partisan lines. As can be expected, the scholars of the University of Paris tended to favor the French Pope Clement; universities in countries loyal to Rome tended to favor the Roman claim.

As you can see, the schism split Christendom down the middle with the dispute affecting every social and political institution. It threw the Church into chaos: entire national hierarchies supported rival papal claimants, each of whom anathematized the followers of the other. It is hard to comprehend what level of spiritual damage this must have caused.

But who was the real pope and who was the antipope? The question was tricky, because unlike the cases of previous antipopes, both claimants were elected by the cardinals. And the supporters of Clement did have a point: according to the Church's canon law, fear of violence could indeed invalidate something like a papal election under the right circumstances.

Despite these uncertainties, the Church's most eminent canon lawyers tended to support the claims of Urban VI. While the Roman mob had pressured the conclave of 1378 to choose an Italian, their intimidation did not reach the levels necessary to nullify the cardinals' free choice in selecting Pope Urban. Furthermore, it was the full College of Cardinals who elected Urban, but only a small remnant consisting of the French cardinals who had chosen Clement VII. Finally, there was no precedent in Church history for a segment of the College of Cardinals (such as those gathered at Anagni in 1378) simply nullifying a papal election on their own authority. The Church has thus always viewed the Roman line of Urban VI as the legitimate popes; the popes of the Avignon obedience have been considered antipopes.

The Schism Continues

The Roman pope, Urban VI, died in 1389 and was replaced with Pope Boniface IX. The Avignon claimant, Clement VII, lived on until 1394. When he died, the Avignon cardinals held another conclave and elected the Spaniard Pedro de Luna, who took the name Benedict XIII. This irritated King Charles VI of France, who wanted the Avignon cardinals to elect a French pope. Charles soon withdrew France's obedience to the Avignon claimant and recognized Boniface IX as the legitimate pope. At this point, most of Benedict XIII's cardinals abandoned him; only five remained loyal.

The Roman pope Boniface IX did not live long, dying in 1404. At this point, the cardinals of the Roman Church made a good faith effort to end the schism. They reached out to the Antipope Benedict XIII and offered to refrain from electing a new pope if Benedict would agree to abdicate. This was a way of "wiping the slate clean," so to speak, so that a new pope could be elected with no rival claimants muddying the water. Benedict refused, however, arguing that all the other cardinals had been invalidly ordained and thus had no power to choose a new pope. The cardinals therefore went ahead and held a conclave, electing Pope Innocent IV in 1404.

The election of Innocent IV alarmed Benedict, who realized he was rapidly losing support. He decided on a bold strategy—a military assault on Rome. Leading an army, Benedict began his march south in 1405 but never made it further than Genoa, lacking the men and resources for such a daring attack. Innocent IV died within the year and the Roman cardinals elected Gregory XII in 1406. Benedict XIII returned to Avignon.

The Council of Pisa

At this point the schism had been going on for twenty-eight years. Many were living who could not remember a time without two rival claimants to the papacy.

Support steadily grew for an ecumenical council to settle the schism. Both popes had momentarily considered stepping down, but this came to nothing. The Avignon claimant Pope Benedict XIII was obstinately against any solution to the schism that required his abdication. But Pope Gregory XII of the Roman obedience had his own problems as well. Being a petty man who staffed the Roman Curia with his own relatives, Pope Gregory XII lacked the moral character to bring the schism to a close.

The cardinals debated whether they could summon an ecumenical council without the pope. Some theologians said yes, others said no. In the end, the cardinals decided that the crisis was serious enough that it justified them summoning a council on their own authority. In 1409 they convened the Council of Pisa, which was attended by eighty bishops, twenty-two cardinals, and hundreds of theologians, abbots, and canon lawyers representing both obediences. Notably absent, however, were Pope Gregory XII, Antipope Benedict XIII, or any of their representatives. Both popes had refused to participate in the Council of Pisa, which they regarded as illegal, as it had been summoned without papal approval.

When neither pope showed up at Pisa, the Council declared them deposed and proceeded to elect a new pope, an Italian Pietro Filargo who took the name Alexander V. The Council also encouraged all cardinals to renounce the obediences of Avignon and Rome in order to support the new pope and threatened to condemnations to any who refused to do so.

Three Popes

As you might imagine, neither Pope Gregory XII nor Benedict XIII recognized the right of the Council of Pisa to depose them and neither stepped down. The result was that there were now three obediences, that of Rome, Avignon, and Pisa.

Gregory XII and Benedict XIII both regarded the Council of Pisa as illegal, and there was some merit to this argument. The cardinals gathered at Pisa considered it their indisputable right to convene a general council to put an end to the schism for the good of the Church. It was pointed out, however, that if Gregory and Benedict were doubtful popes, then so were the cardinals whom they had created. And, it followed, if the source of those cardinals' authority was uncertain, so was their jurisdiction to convoke the Council of Pisa and to elect a new pope. How then could Alexander V, elected by doubtful cardinals, claim the indisputable allegiance of all Christendom?

Antipope Alexander V only reigned for one year before his death in 1410, at which point the cardinals elected a successor, Baldassare Cossa, who took the name John XXIII.

The Council of Constance

The election of Antipope John XXIII worsened the crisis considerably, as it signaled the perpetuation of the Pisan line begun by Alexander V. John, however, was not unaware of the danger the Church was now in with three obediences and was resolved to do his part to end the crisis. If the Pisan pope and Roman pope both jointly endorsed a council, it would enjoy greater legitimacy. John XXIII, therefore, summoned the Council of Constance in 1414 and Gregory XII authorized it as well. Both popes also agreed that the Council of Constance would possess the authority to settle the schism. The Council was supported by Sigismund, King of Germany, who was also determined to end the controversy.

The Council argued that all three popes should resign so a new one could be elected. The Roman pope, Gregory XII, agreed. John was hesitant to resign, however, and fled Constance disguised as a postman. King Sigismund was furious at John's attempt to perpetuate the schism and sent soldiers to capture the truant pope. John XXIII took refuge with the Duke of Austria, but the Duke handed him over to the king's men, who imprisoned John in Germany for the duration of the Council.

With John XXIII safely imprisoned, the Council declared him deposed. Gregory XII resigned as promised. As for the Avignon claimant Benedict XIII, he remained obstinate in his refusal. By this time, however, the Avignon obedience had been reduced considerably and Benedict was

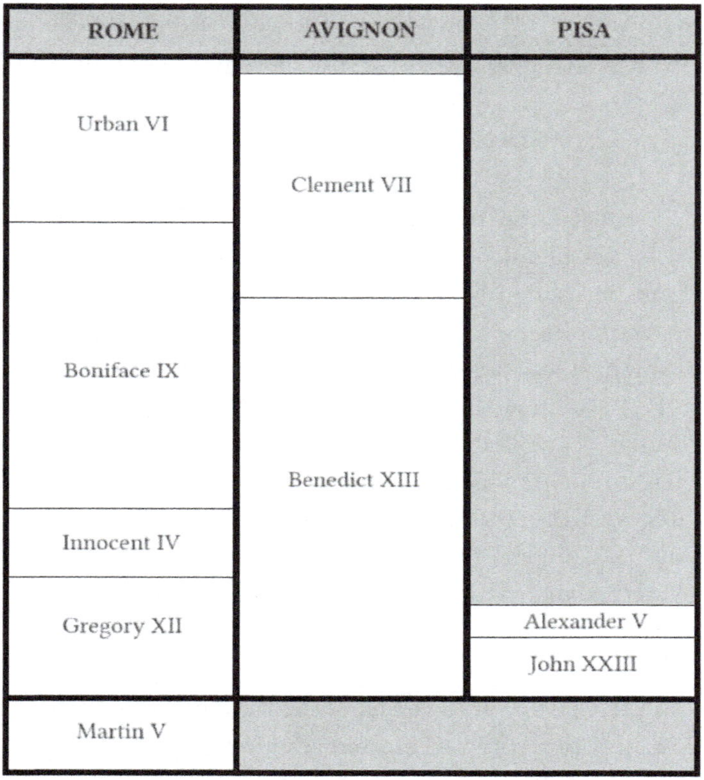

Graph depicting the overlapping tenures of the papal claimants from the three lines. The schism ended with the resignation of Gregory XII, the deposition of the two antipopes at the Council of Constance, and the election of Martin V in 1417

no longer considered a serious threat to unity. The Council excommunicated him.

With all three papal claimants resigned or deposed, a conclave was summoned to elect a new pope—Martin V, the first undisputed pope in thirty-nine years. As for John XXIII, he was released from captivity and made his submission to Pope Martin, who made him Cardinal Bishop of Frasati.

The Fate of Pope Luna's Obedience

The Spaniard Pedro de Luna, the Avignon antipope Benedict XIII, came to a sad end. Driven out of Avignon and hounded by King Sigismund, Pedro fled to Tortosa in Valencia with his ever-dwindling handful of supporters. There he set up a tiny papal court and continued to put on the airs of the papacy, supported by nobody save King Alfonso V of Aragon, who continued to humor the old antipope until his death in 1423.

Pedro de Luna considered himself the true pope till his dying day. Shortly before death, he appointed four cardinals to carry on his succession. Those cardinals in turn held a conclave to elect a successor, Antipope Clement VIII. Clement's election was contested even among those four, however, and a second man was elected, taking the name Benedict XIV. Thus a fresh schism broke out among the tiny sect of Pedro de Luna's succession. Clement VIII renounced his claims and was reconciled with Rome in 1429, effectively ending the Luna obedience. The other claimant, Benedict XIV, had the support of only one single prelate, Jean Carrier, one of Luna's four cardinals. When Benedict died in 1430, Carrier elected himself Benedict's successor and bizarrely chose the same name, Benedict XIV. This

Benedict was captured, however, and spent the rest of his days in captivity. When he died in 1437, the line of Pedro de Luna was definitively ended.

Effects of the Western Schism

The effects of the Western Schism on the Catholic Church were profound and overwhelmingly negative.

In the short term, the confusion of the Western Schism led to the rise of a movement known as Conciliarism. The scandal of multiple rival papal claimants caused many theologians to question whether the pope was truly the supreme authority in the Church. After all, had not the drama of the schism demonstrated the shortcomings of papal supremacy? Some would argue that a council was superior to the pope. These were called Conciliarists. The Conciliarists attempted to enforce legislation binding popes to call regular councils, as well as pressured later popes to admit the superiority of ecumenical councils. The popes resisted this attack on their authority. The result was decades of infighting amongst theologians over the limits of papal authority. In 1460, Pope Pius II issued the bull *Execrabilis*, forbidding anyone to appeal papal judgments to general councils. Conciliarism was condemned as a heresy in 1516 during the Fifth Lateran Council—a mere ten months before Martin Luther launched the Protestant Reformation.

In the long term, the Western Schism eroded papal authority. The days of papal utterances bringing kings and emperors to knee were long gone. During the decades of the schism, rival popes appealed to the kings of Christendom to support their claims. This effectively strengthened the monarchs of Europe at the expense of the papacy by indebting the popes to royal power. The climate of acrimony and contention between papal courts—with rival claimants condemning and issuing excommunications against one another—weakened papal authority and cheapened the effectiveness of excommunication as a discipline. In this climate it is not surprising that clerical discipline also suffered. Many tracts written throughout the 1400s complained about the poor state of the clergy. By the turn of the 16th century the Church had begun to reform itself, but by that time the Protestant Reformation was only a few years away. Indeed, many historians consider the Western Schism an important precursor to the Protestant Reformation, as Martin Luther's attacks on papal authority were anticipated in the arguments of the Conciliarists. In effect, the Western Schism fractured the unity of the medieval Church and sowed doubt in the mind of Christendom about the Church as an institution.

The Schism and Papal Infallibility

The Western Schism was a very bad time for the Church. There really is no silver lining to be found amidst its intricate and divisive disputes.

That being said, did the schism have any bearing on the idea of papal infallibility? After all, if the Church had three popes contradicting and excommunicating one another, how could we still affirm an infallible papacy?

We ought to remember that there never were truly two or three popes reigning simultaneously. We speak of "three popes" out of convention, but in reality we are dealing with multiple claimants to the papacy, only one of whom could ever be authentic, as there cannot be more than one pope reigning at a time. During the schism, then, what we really had was one real pope and one (or two) antipopes. The Church recognizes the Roman obedience as the authentic succession. Papal infallibility really doesn't come into play here, as none of the acts of the antipopes possessed the charism of infallibility.

Furthermore, papal infallibility is considerably more restrictive than many people think. It does not mean the pope will never make a prudential error, nor that the pope won't behave poorly, nor that he won't sin or scandalize the faithful. It means, rather, that the Holy Spirit restricts him from teaching erroneously under very specific circumstances: when he speaks in his official capacity as supreme pastor of the Church on matters of faith or morals that he wishes to bind the entire Church to affirm.[6] As none of the four legitimate popes during the schism even made such declarations, it is a moot point to invoke papal infallibility at all in reference to the schism.

Thus, while the Western Schism was certainly a time of trouble for the Church, none of these tumults has any bearing on papal infallibility.

What to Do with a Corrupt Pope?

Finally, the Western Schism calls to mind the perennial problem of what to do with a corrupt pope. Multiple times during the schism, the cardinals were faced with papal claimants—of various lines—that, for one reason or another, they wished to be rid of. Some, like Gregory XII, were openly charged with nepotism and corruption. What can the Church do about a corrupt pope who is scandalizing the faithful and wounding the unity of the Church?

Pope Martin V (r. 1417-1431). His uncontested election after the Council of Constance signaled the end of the Western Schism

The Catholic Church affirms the canonical principle *prima sedes a nemine iudicatur*, which means, "The first see is judged by no one." This means the Roman pontiff has no earthly superior; there is no individual or body that can pass judgment on him, discipline him, or depose him.

That being said, that's not to say that the Church is powerless in the face of a hypothetically corrupt or evil pope. Thomas Cajetan (1469-1534), one of the greatest theologians in the century after the schism, wrote extensively on this question. Cajetan argued that, in the first place, Christians ought to have recourse to God to pray that He would deliver His Church from an evil pontiff. Cajetan wrote:

> It does not follow from the fact that the Church has not been granted the power to depose by human provision that it has not been granted [any] power to depose a pope; for it does so unfailingly by another means, namely, by persevering in prayer...If nature does not fail in what is necessary, how can God, who gave Himself to the Church, fail her in necessary things, if the Church has done what it ought to do, as is obvious from the conditions of prayer described?[7]

Beyond this, Cajetan says Christians should resist a pope if he attempts to use his powers for wickedness (for example, if the pope were to use his office to steal or give away Church offices to his relatives, etc.). Cajetan says:

> You must resist, therefore, to his face a pope who openly is tearing the Church apart, for example, because he refuses to grant ecclesiastical offices

> except for money, or in exchange for an office...and a case of simony, even committed by the pope, must be denounced. Without a doubt [if even] secular princes and the clergy could properly take the sword from a madman's hand...Let them meet with fitting remedies the destructive abuse of power by not obeying the wicked, not flattering, not being silent, by accusing, by arguing, summoning the princes to rebuke, following Paul's example...[If they would do this] he would abuse power little, or not at all.[8]

While we must always heed every legitimate command of the Roman pontiff in his governance of the Church, we should also recall the words of the Apostles, "We ought to obey God rather than men," (Acts 5:29). The duty of obedience never extends into the realm of sin, whether committing it ourselves, or empowering others to do so.

Conclusion

Every family has embarrassing episodes. Most of us have had drama within our households or extended families that would be awkward to discuss with outsiders. The Church, of course, is the family of God (CCC 1565), and like any family, the Church has had its own share of family drama and internal squabbling. The Western Schism was one such episode.

Any schism is a cause for regret, as it wounds the unity of the Church, and all Catholics should regret the divisions that arose out of the Western Schism. If anything, the schism highlights the importance of having clear canonical procedures for the confusing circumstances that can arise at sensitive times, like the election or resignation of a pontiff. It also demonstrates that, even with the guidance of the Holy Spirit, there are still plenty of ways that human prudence can fail and make a mess of things. We can see why Thomas Cajetan advocated so strongly for Christians to turn to prayer in bad times. When human judgment fails, let our recourse always be to God, who never fails to give the Church what it needs in due season.

The keys of St. Peter, emblem of the papacy

For Further Reading

Cantor, Norman. *Medieval History: The Life and Death of a Civilization*. 2nd edition. Macmillan: London, 1971.

Conciliarism and Papalism, ed. by J.H. Burns and Thomas Izbicki. Cambridge University Press: Cambridge, 1998.

Huzinga, Johan. *The Waning of the Middle Ages: A Study of the Forms of Life, Thought and Art in France and the Netherlands in the XIVth and XVth Centuries.* Edward Arnold & Co: London, 1924.

Kitts, Eustace. *In the Days of the Councils: A Sketch of the Life and Times of Baldassare Cossa*. Archibald Constable and Co.: London, 1908.

Stuart, Joseph & Barbara. *The Church and the Age of Reformations* (1350-1650). Ave Maria Press: Notre Dame, IN., 2020

Weidenkopf, Steve. *Timeless: A History of the Catholic Church.* Our Sunday Visitor: Huntington, IN., 2019.

Notes

[1] St. Cyprian of Carthage, *On the Unity of the Church*, 5

[2] See "Baby Jesus and the Universal Christian Church or the New Jerusalem", available online at https://magnuslundbergblog.wordpress.com/wp-content/uploads/2020/07/bambino-gesu-finished4.pdf

[3] Andrea Galgliarducci, "Schismatic sect in Italy incurs excommunication," *Catholic News Agency*, June 6, 2016. See https://www.catholicnewsagency.com/news/33996/schismatic-sect-in-italy-incurs-excommunication

[4] Another claimant, antipope Innocent III, was proclaimed by the pro-Imperial families of Tusculum in 1178 but he was quickly defeated and imprisoned in 1180.

[5] Johan Huizinga, *The Waning of the Middle Ages: A Study of the Forms of Life, Thought and Art in France and the Netherlands in the XIVth and XVth Centuries* (Edward Arnold & Co: London, 1924), 14

[6] See the First Vatican Council's *Pastor Aeternus*, as well as the *Catechism of the Catholic Church* § 891

[7] Thomas Cajetan, *Apology*, Cap. VI, in *Conciliarism and Papalism*, ed. by J.H. Burns and Thomas Izbicki (Cambridge University Press: Cambridge, 1998) 282-284

[8] Ibid., *De comparatione*, Cap. XXVII

Printed in Dunstable, United Kingdom

63978701R00020